Study G

Youth Edition

T·H·E
BONDAGE BREAKER

Neil T. Anderson
& Dave Park

HARVEST HOUSE PUBLISHERS
Eugene, Oregon 97402

Scripture quotations in this book are taken from the New American Standard Bible, © 1960, 1962, 1963, 1968, 1971, 1972, 1973, 1975, 1977 by The Lockman Foundation. Used by permission.

THE BONDAGE BREAKER YOUTH EDITION STUDY GUIDE

Copyright © 1995 by Harvest House Publishers
Eugene, Oregon 97402

ISBN 1-56507-293-6

Printed in the United States of America.

98 99 00 — 10 9 8 7 6 5 4 3

Contents

Preface

Part One: Take Courage!

Part Two: Stand Firm!

Part Three: Walk Free!

Preface

One of the best ways to know God better is to get into His Word, the Bible. And reading Christian books and study guides like this one is a great way to strengthen your walk with Him.

Before you begin each lesson, take time to pray and ask God to teach you new truths about Him. Ephesians 1:18-21 says, "I pray that the eyes of your heart may be enlightened, so that you may know what is the hope of His calling, what are the riches of the glory of His inheritance in the saints, and what is the surpassing greatness of His power toward us who believe. These are in accordance with the working of the strength of His might which He brought about in Christ, when He raised Him from the dead, and seated Him at His right hand in the heavenly places, far above all rule and authority and power and dominion, and every name that is named, not only in this age, but also in the one to come."

Like Paul the apostle, we (Neil and Dave) are praying that as you study God's Word, the eyes of your heart will be open to the hope of your calling, your inheritance, and your authority in Christ. And remember—you are not just studying *The Bondage Breaker Youth Edition Study Guide*, but *Jesus*, who is your Bondage Breaker.

1

You Don't Have to Live in the Shadows

Are You Living in the Shadows?

Dear God,
   Where are You? How can You watch and not help me? I hurt so bad, and You don't even care. If You cared, You'd make it stop or let me die. I love You, but You seem so far away. I can't hear You or feel You or see You, but I'm supposed to believe You're here....

You may have asked these very questions and felt some of these feelings yourself. The woman who wrote these words before she unsuccessfully tried to commit suicide may be voicing pain that you've felt. If so, know that the message of this chapter—and this book—is that you don't have to live in the shadows created by such dark thoughts.

- Your darkness may not involve voices in your head. Many Christians don't complain about hearing voices, but they will say that their daily walk with Christ is really discouraging. When they try to pray, they begin thinking about the million things they should be doing. When they sit down to read the Bible or a book by a Christian author, they can't concentrate. When they have an opportunity to serve the Lord, they are overwhelmed by self-doubt ("I'm not a strong enough Christian"; "I don't know enough about the Bible"), so they don't even try.

— Which of these struggles do you face? Where, if at all, are you discouraged in your Christian walk?

— The kind of discouragement described above can come from our own faulty thinking, but it can also be a sign that the enemy is attacking. How might the enemy be deceiving you right now? In what area of your life might he be trying to keep you from growing?

Whether or not you are hearing voices in your head (and many of the young people we surveyed do), you need to know how to defend yourself against Satan's fiery darts, whatever shape they come in. So keep reading.

Common False Beliefs about Bondage

• First, what do you think about when you hear the

word "bondage"? What do you feel when you hear that word?

• The evil voices, guilty feelings, and confusion you read about in *The Bondage Breaker Youth Edition* are ways that Satan can keep us in bondage. And one reason he is able to do so is because we don't understand the spiritual world. Review pages 20-25 in the text, the discussion of the false beliefs listed below.

1. Demons were busy when Christ was on earth, but they're not around much today.

   What does Paul's warning in Ephesians 6:12-17 suggest about how busy demons are or aren't today?

   What evidence do you see of demon activity today?

2. What early Christians called demonic activity is only mental illness.

   Why would many psychologists never bring up the possibility of demonic activity?

Why is Satan the deceiver pleased with this fact?

3. Some problems are psychological and some are spiritual.

   Why can't we draw a line like this between our psyche (our mind) and our spirit?

   When have you personally been aware of the indivisible connection between your heart, your mind, your spirit, and your body?

4. Christians can't be attacked by demonic forces.

   Again, what does Paul's warning in Ephesians 6:12-17 say that proves the statement above is wrong?

   And, again, why is Satan the deceiver pleased with the popularity of this false idea?

5. The activity of demons is only seen in weird behavior or gross sin.

How does Satan benefit from this misunderstanding of his activity?

What does Paul's teaching in 2 Corinthians 11:14,15 suggest about the shape of demon influence?

6. Freedom from spiritual bondage is the result of a power encounter with demonic forces.

What does Neil's boyhood experience with the farm dog teach you about Satan's activity?

What is significant to you about the fact that a truth encounter—not a power encounter—is what leads to freedom from spiritual bondage?

• Which of the false ideas listed above have you encountered? If you accepted any of them as true, how has doing so affected your life?

- Take time to read God's truth. What do the following verses say about Satan and Christ?

  — John 8:44

  — John 10:10

  — John 14:6

- What have you learned so far about the reality of the spiritual world? In three or four sentences, sum up what the Bible teaches about the spiritual world.

Satan deceives us. His power is in the lie: He wants you and me to believe and live a lie. As a Christian, however, you have the power that comes with knowing the truth. When you believe, declare, and act on the truth you find in God's Word, you ruin Satan's strategy and find freedom.

Setting Captives Free

Something radical happened at the cross and in the resurrection that permanently changed the way we encounter spiritual forces.

- First, in His death and resurrection, Jesus defeated and disarmed the rulers of darkness (Colossians 2:15) and was given all authority "in heaven and on earth"

(Matthew 28:18). Because of the cross, Satan is defeated; he has no authority over those who are in Christ. Second, in Christ's death and resurrection, every believer is made alive with Him and resides in Him.

— What do these truths say about how you can respond when Satan harasses you?

— The next time you're feeling hassled by Satan, how will you respond? What will you do to exercise your position and authority in Christ? Be specific.

— If you want to learn more about standing strong against Satan, to whom will you go for help?

• Since you are in Christ, you never again need to live in the shadows. Instead, from your position in Christ, you are responsible for choosing the truth and resisting the devil. You are responsible for renouncing (turning your back on) the ways you have participated in his scheme. (We'll discuss this in greater detail in Part Three.)

— At this point, what behaviors do you need to confess as wrong and stop doing?

— What attitudes (pride, hard-heartedness, envy, and so on) do you need to renounce and release?

— And to whom do you need to extend forgiveness?

We are able to choose the truth and resist the devil because of who we are in Christ, and fully understanding God's provision for you in Christ is key to understanding how He can be your bondage breaker.

• "A Lost Sheep" came to a better understanding of who she is in Christ. Turn to page 28 of the text and read again the letter she wrote in response to her own earlier cry for help.

— Which words of truth do you especially need to hear right now? Write them out below and know that they are indeed God's words to you.

— What words of hope from this letter do you want to believe with your heart as well as your head? Ask God to help you believe.

The truth of who you are in Jesus Christ is the light which can and will dispel the shadows in your life.

A Step toward Freedom

Here and throughout the study guide, you'll have a chance to take a step toward freedom. Since freedom comes from Jesus, the Bondage Breaker, and His truth, the steps will involve Scripture and prayer.

• Which of the following verses is an especially effective reminder of the truth that God's love and power in the cross is what frees us from Satan's grip? Write out the verse you choose on an index card and memorize it.

— John 14:6

— John 17:15,17

— Philippians 4:8

— Romans 8:38,39

— 1 Peter 3:21b,22

- Spend a few minutes in prayer and ask God to help you recognize any misunderstanding you might have about Him, Satan, and the spiritual world. Then ask the Lord to replace those false ideas with His truth. You might also ask Him to provide a more mature believer (such as a pastor or youth leader) who can help guide you to a better understanding of God's truth. Also, if you are feeling as if you could have written the letter by "A Lost Sheep," find someone trustworthy you can share your feelings with and have that person pray with you and for you during these dark days. Finally, ask God to help you grow in your understanding of who you are in Christ.

2

Finding Your Way in the World

Have You Been Caught in Satan's Web?

- In his novel *Lord of the Flies*, what does William Golding propose is the source of evil in the world? Why does Satan not interfere with this idea?

- What does Dave's description of the chicken he found waiting for him after his three-week trip suggest to you about Satan's strategy in the world?

- Perhaps you have unknowingly entered into Satan's realm. Today's popular culture innocently offers many avenues. Which of the following, if any, have you "played with" or enjoyed but never taken seriously?

  Dungeons & Dragons
  Ouija boards

Movies like *Ghostbusters, Field of Dreams,
  Ghost, Poltergeist, The Exorcist Hell Raisers*
Palm-reading
New Age ideas (channeling, spirit guides)

Satan—the one who lures people into his trap through parapsychology, the culture's fascination with the supernatural, and the popularizing of Ouija boards, astrology, Dungeons & Dragons, and palm-reading—would like us to believe that he doesn't really exist and that evil is just a human weakness.

The Two-Level Worldview

The word "worldview" refers to how you understand the world around you, how you relate to it, and what you believe about reality. But neither the two-level Western worldview nor the two-level Eastern worldview (both described in the text on pages 34-35) reflects the truth of the Bible.

- Missions expert Dr. Paul Hiebert points to something between the seen world of the senses and the unseen world of God and spiritual forces and calls it the "excluded middle." What happens in this excluded middle, which is excluded from our minds only because we choose to ignore it?

- Remember Dee? She learned that the real world includes spiritual forces which are active in the seen, physical world. What did you learn from Dee's experience?

- Do you, like Dee's father, tend not to consider the possibility of spiritual causes for physical ailments? What can result from not considering the possible spiritual root of physical problems?

When we exclude the supernatural from our worldview or believe it has no effect on our lives, we exclude God's power from our beliefs and practices. We also tend to explain all human problems as resulting from mental or physical causes rather than spiritual ones.

Living in the Excluded Middle

- Scripture clearly teaches that supernatural forces are at work in the world. What do the following passages teach about those forces?

  — Mark 5:1-20

  — Luke 13:11,12

  — Ephesians 6:12

- Neil and Dave encourage you to see both your doctor, who will test and treat you physically, *and* your pastor, who should be able to test and treat you spiritually. Why is this balanced approach reasonable and important?

Getting Spiritual Without God

Unsatisfied by the materialistic world as well as unhappy with organized religion, many people today turn to the occult, Eastern religions, and New Age ideas to try to fill their spiritual emptiness. In other words, they try to get spiritual without God.

- When God is not at the center of our lives, who steps in?

- When we become our own god, what happens to our primary concerns?

- In Matthew 16:13-23, how does the apostle Peter illustrate the struggle between living for self and living for Christ?

- In what areas of your life do you especially struggle with living for Christ instead of for yourself?

Satan's primary aim is to get us to center our lives on our own interests—"Save yourself at all costs! Watch out for yourself! Don't do anything that is painful or inconvenient!" But the Christian looks at life from a different perspective: Ours is the view from the cross.

The View from the Cross

This view shatters Satan's lie that we human beings can be our own god. We were not designed to be gods, and we will never be gods. We must replace the false idea that we can be gods (popularized in this generation by the New Age movement) with the teachings of Jesus. The following six guidelines, based on Jesus' words in Matthew 16:24-27, will free you from the bondage of the world system and the devil who inspires it. These guidelines will help you find your way in a dark world.

Deny Yourself

- Explain how denying yourself is not the same as self-denial. Consider, for starters, the ultimate purpose of each.

- Why is denying yourself essential to spiritual freedom?

Pick Up Your Cross Daily

- What has the cross of Christ provided for believers? See, for instance, John 3:16 and 2 Corinthians 5:21.

- What does the phrase "pick up your cross" mean? Be specific—and remember that the cross we're referring to is Christ's cross.

Follow Christ

- Where will the path of following Christ lead you? Does that destination sound good? Why or why not?

- Only when you have come to the end of your resources (died to self-rule) will you discover God's resources. What will such an experience teach you? What will you gain?

The instruction to deny yourself, pick up your cross daily, and follow Christ may sound as if you are sacrificing yourself and gaining nothing. But consider now what you're sacrificing and what you're gaining.

Sacrifice the Lower Life to Gain the Higher Life

- How are you trying to save your natural life? Are you trying to find your identity and sense of worth in positions, titles, grades, friends, accomplishments, or possessions? How is pursuing these things interfering with your pursuit of spiritual things?

- If you shoot for this world, that's all you'll get—and eventually you'll lose even that. But if you shoot for the next world, God will throw this one in as a bonus (1 Timothy 4:8). What can you do to shoot for the next world instead of this one? Be specific.

Sacrifice the Pleasure of Things to Gain the Pleasure of Life

- Identify two or three ways the world says that fame and possessions will bring you love, joy, peace, and patience—that is, the fruit of God's Spirit (Galatians 5:22,23). Which worldly pleasures have you looked to for love, joy, peace, and patience?

- Read Luke 10:38-42. What was Martha interested in? What was Mary interested in? Are you more like Martha, loving things, or Mary, loving God and people? Support your answer with specific evidence from your life.

Sacrifice the Temporary to Gain the Eternal

- Look again at Hebrews 11:24-26. What did Moses sacrifice? What did he hope to gain by doing so?

- What temporary things are you sacrificing—or could you sacrifice—to gain the eternal rewards of heaven?

Whenever you live independently of God, focusing on yourself instead of Christ, seeking material and worldly things over spiritual and eternal things, Satan couldn't be more pleased. After all, he wants to take God's place in your life by convincing you that you can be your own God.

A Step toward Freedom

- Again, read Matthew 16:24-27.

  — What are some practical ways you can pick up your cross daily and follow Jesus?

  — Why do we have so much trouble denying ourselves and following Christ? What role can prayer play in enabling us to pick up the cross each day and follow Jesus?

- Ask God to show you what He would have you do to deny yourself...pick up your cross...and follow Him more closely. Ask Him to give you a deeper longing for the higher life rather than the lower life...greater desire for the pleasure of life in Him rather than pleasure in worldly things...and greater hunger for things eternal rather than the temporary things of the world. Then close your prayer by asking Him to teach you how to live each moment with Him on the throne of your life.

3

You Have Every Right to Be Free

A Dearly Loved Child of God

- Answer the two questions Neil asked Lydia: "Who are you?" and, "How do you see yourself?"

- Satan had deceived Lydia into believing she was worthless and evil. Has he deceived you or do your answers above reflect a solid understanding of who you are in Christ?

Nothing is more basic to our freedom from Satan's bondage than understanding what God has done for us in Christ and who we are as a result. If you see yourself as the dearly loved and accepted child of God that you really are, your attitudes, actions, and responses to life's circumstances will be very different than if you see yourself as evil and worthless. In this chapter, we'll look closely at who we are in Christ. Believe these words of truth! They are for you!

You Are Eternally Alive
and Well

When we were born again, our soul/spirit was united with God and we came alive spiritually. And this spiritual life we have received in Christ is eternal.

- Read Ephesians 1:1-14, noticing especially verses 7 and 13. What is your standing in relation to Christ once you accept Him as your Savior and Lord?

- What promise, quoted in Hebrews 13:5, guarantees the security of the eternal life you have in Christ?

- What causes you to doubt your relationship with Christ? With what truth in the Bible can you answer and dispel that idea, which comes straight from Satan himself?

You Are Changed
from Sinner to Saint

Christians who consider themselves "just sinners saved by grace" tend to be defeated Christians rather than victorious, effective believers.

• Do you see yourself as a sinner or a saint? Explain.

• Why does seeing ourselves as sinners—even sinners saved by grace—often lead to despair and more sinning?

• How can seeing yourself as a saint—who sometimes sins—help you stand strong against sin and Satan? What specific truths from the Bible can also help you?

You Have Been Given God's Divine Nature

Ephesians 2:1-3 describes our nature before we came to Christ: Our nature was sin, and the result of our sin was death (separation from God). But at salvation God changed us: We received His divine nature (2 Peter 1:4; 2 Corinthians 5:17; Ephesians 5:8).

• How have your thoughts, words, and actions changed since you became a Christian? How does your behavior reflect the fact that you are a new creature in Christ (2 Corinthians 5:17)?

- Being a new creation in Christ doesn't mean being sinless. What sins do you battle? Where are you choosing to act independently of God?

- How does the fact that you are a partaker of God's divine nature encourage you in your walk of faith, despite your sins?

You Can Be Victorious
Over the Flesh and Sin

When our old sinful self died, sin's rule as our master ended. But sin is still around. Even though sin's power and authority have been broken (Romans 8:2), sin remains strong and appealing. It is our responsibility not to let sin rule in our body.

- Look again at Romans 6:12,13. What is God commanding you specifically?

- What peer pressure do you feel to serve sin rather than God with your body? Confess where you have chosen to serve sin.

- What are you doing—or could you be doing—to stand strong against the appeal of sin and the apparent popularity of certain sinful actions? One thing you could be doing is asking God to give you the strength you need to stand firm for what you know is right.

You Can Be Free
from the Power of Sin

In Romans 7:15-25, Paul shares the frustrations that come with battling sin and points to God's path to freedom from the power of sin.

- First, how do you respond to your sinfulness? Do you see yourself as wicked or miserable and enchained? Do you condemn yourself rather than recognizing the role of the "dog" (sin) that is inflicting the pain?

- Perhaps you don't beat yourself up when you sin, but do you take responsibility for your failure? Do you acknowledge the wrong choices you make which lead to sin? Do you see where you are allowing sin to rule in your body? Give a specific example.

- What hope did Paul find in his struggle with sin? What hope do you find for your own battle?

You Can Win the Battle
for Your Mind

The center of all spiritual bondage is the mind (Romans 7:23, 8:5-7). Satan introduces his thoughts, tempting you to act independently of God, as if they were your own thoughts or even God's thoughts.

- When have you seen afterwards that a thought you had or a thought which appeared to come from God probably had its origin with the evil one? What happened and what did you learn from that experience?

- What does the command to take "every thought captive to the obedience of Christ" (2 Corinthians 10:5) mean to you in practical, live-your-life terms?

- Look again at Morgan's story (pages 60-61 of the text).

  — What can you learn from Morgan's experience?

  — Review the nine thoughts Morgan had as she battled the temptation to vomit. Which of these statements can you add to your arsenal so that you'll be able to stand strong in the battle the next time you're facing the temptation to do something that will not glorify God?

Victory over temptation—freedom from bondage to Satan—is truly available for those who are in Christ. There is a war raging, but you are on the winning side, for you are more than a conqueror in Christ!

A Step toward Freedom

• Look at pages 220-225 in the text, which list the Bible's answers to the question, Who am I? Choose one or two passages to memorize as reminders of who you are in Christ.

• Ask God to open your eyes so that you can see clearly the strongholds in your life—those thought patterns, bad habits, and ongoing behaviors which don't honor God and which keep you from experiencing the freedom available to you, His child. Also, ask God to show you the truth about who you are in Him so that you, like Morgan, will be able to stand strong in Christ against Satan's temptations. Finally, thank God that freedom from Satan's deception is indeed available to you because of the sacrificial act of His Son and your Savior Jesus Christ.

4
Confronting the Rebel Prince

Resisting the Devil

- What does James 4:7 say? What does James 4:7 suggest will happen if we don't resist Satan?

- Initially, Daisy was reluctant to call on the name of Christ and command the snakes to leave. Why was she hesitant? What did Neil teach Daisy about why she was able to issue such a command?

Resisting the devil is your responsibility based on the authority you possess in Christ.

Carrying Jesus' Badge of Authority

As you learn to use your authority over the kingdom of darkness, consider the warning Jesus gave His disciples. It's also a warning for you!

- Read Luke 9:1,2. What did Jesus give His disciples to equip them for ministry? According to Luke 10:17, how effective were the disciples?

- In Luke 10:19,20, what did Jesus say is far more important than having authority over evil powers?

Jesus is calling His disciples—which includes you and me today—to be God-centered, not demon-centered. It is God's truth that sets us free, not how much we know about Satan and his lies.

The Right and the Ability

- Authority is the *right* to rule. Power is the *ability* to rule.

  — Why do we believers need both the right and the ability in our battle against Satan?

  — What does the story of David and Goliath (see 1 Samuel 17) teach you about your ability to resist Satan and his demons?

When you encounter the spiritual Goliaths which are fighting against your soul, look at them in relation to

your great and powerful God and then triumph as David
did.

Pulling Rank

- Too often, we mistakenly see God and His kingdom
  on one side and Satan and his kingdom on the other
  side and us stuck in the middle, like the rope in a
  game of tug-of-war.

  — Spiritual authority does not involve a game of
    tug-of-war. What chain of command does the
    Bible outline? (See Matthew 28:18 and Luke 10:17.)

  — If Jesus Christ has all authority in heaven and on
    earth and He has given that authority to His chil-
    dren to be used in His name, why does the
    kingdom of darkness exercise such a powerful
    evil influence in the world and in the lives of
    many Christians? (Hint: Satan is also known as
    the deceiver.)

In Christ, you have been given authority over the kingdom of darkness, but if you don't believe that truth and
use that authority—if you believe Satan's lies instead—
it's as if you don't have it.

Jesus' Badge of Authority in Today's World

Paul has some exciting news for believers in the opening
lines of his letter to the Ephesians. May we have eyes to
see and hearts to believe!

- Christians today enjoy the same claim to Christ's authority in the spiritual world as His twelve disciples did. But what advantage do we have over those twelve?

- The first disciples were *with* Christ (Mark 3:14,15), but we are *in* Christ (Ephesians 1:3-13). Look again at Ephesians 1:18-20. What is Paul's heartfelt prayer for believers like us? List the requests he lays before God.

- How would your life be different if you really understood what it means to be in Christ? Consider, for instance, the power that Paul describes in his prayer—power that is available to you who are in Christ.

How are we Christians ever going to get our job done in the world if we don't believe what God says about the kingdom of darkness and about the authority and re-responsibility we have in Christ?

Do You Have What It Takes?

Saying we believe is not enough. We must act. We must put into use Christ's authority over spiritual powers. Every believer has spiritual authority because of his or her position in Christ. But there are at least four qualifications for exercising authority over rulers and authorities in the spiritual world.

1. Belief—If you, a Christian, don't believe you have authority, you're not going to exercise it. If your belief is weak, your expression of it will also be weak and ineffective.

   — What belief is fundamental to breaking the bondage of Satan? Why is that belief crucial?

   — Evaluate your belief. Are you completely confident that, in Christ, you have authority over Satan and his powers? On what points are you less than 100 percent confident? What will you do to grow in your faith?

Build your faith in your authority in Christ by studying how Jesus operated against the powers of darkness in the Gospels and how we are commanded to do so in the Epistles.

2. Humility—This virtue of the Christian faith is hardly respected in our modern world.

   — How do you define "humility"?

   — Humility is confidence properly placed. Give an example of how Jesus modeled humility. Then explain why humility is key to exercising authority in the spiritual world.

True humility says, "I resisted the devil by the grace of God." We exercise authority humbly in Christ's strength and His name.

3. Boldness—A Spirit-controlled Christian has a true, godly sense of courage and boldness in spiritual warfare.

   — What is the opposite of boldness?

   — Where do you fall on the spectrum ranging from boldness to cowardice? What encouragement toward boldness do you find in 2 Timothy 1:7?

Christians whose faith in the Lord is vibrant and growing need not fear the dark side of the spiritual world. After all, God has given us a spirit of power (2 Timothy 1:7).

4. Dependence—Remember that the authority we're talking about is not independent authority. Ours is an authority given to us and directed by God.

   — God does not call you and me to be Christian ghostbusters trying to hunt down the devil. What is God's primary call to His people? What specifically are you doing in response to that call?

   — The kingdom ministry of loving, caring, preaching, teaching, praying, and sharing the good news is to be our focus. When, then, are we to exercise our authority over Satan? And on whom are we to depend when we do so?

Whenever we are doing God's kingdom work and demonic powers challenge us, we deal with them on the basis of our authority in Christ and our dependence on Him. God's light dispels Satan's darkness. God's truth exposes the lie.

The Bottom Line: Freedom

Satan can do nothing about your position in Christ. But he will try to cloud your beliefs and confuse you. He will try to make you forget who you are in Christ so that he can defeat you in spiritual battle.

- How might Satan be trying to cloud your beliefs? Are you, for instance, confused about your standing in Christ? What will you do to gain a better understanding?

- Why does confusion or diminished faith mean less effectiveness and even total defeat in battle?

When we boldly and humbly exercise the authority that Christ has given us over spiritual powers, we experience the freedom from bondage which Christ promises (John 8:32).

A Step toward Freedom

- The truths of Matthew 28:18 and Luke 10:17 are truths for your daily life. Keep them in mind as, below, you list the four qualifications for doing effective spiritual battle. What will you do this week to strengthen each of these qualities in your life? Be specific.

• Thank God for the authority and the power over Satan's darkness which, as a believer, you have in Christ Jesus. Ask Him to open your eyes so that you can more fully understand just what it means that Christ has extended you power and authority over Satan. Then ask God to teach you to exercise that authority and power with faith, humility, boldness, and dependence on Him.

5

Jesus Has You Covered

Gaining an Enemy

• Have you noticed that your life as a Christian is tougher than your life B.C. (before Christ)? Point to an example or two and then explain why many Christians have found life more difficult since naming Christ as their Lord and Savior.

• Some Christians are a little paranoid about evil powers. But we needn't feel that way.

— What do you know about germs and how they work? What does this knowledge prompt you to do?

— Aware of germs, we wisely become health-conscious. We eat the right foods, get plenty of rest, and keep clean. If we happen to catch a cold, we simply deal with it and go on with life. Explain what a similar approach to demons would be like. What would you focus on? What health-conscious moves would you make for your spiritual well-being?

Aware of demons, we wisely become Christ-centered. We commit ourselves to living a righteous life. Should we come under attack, we deal with it and go on. In Jesus, we are equipped with all the authority and protection we need to deal with anything that comes our way.

Getting Involved in God's Protection

Ephesians 6:10-18 tells us all about God's protection program and identifies our role in implementing its benefits.

- List the commands in Ephesians 6:10-13 which demand action on your part.

- Why must you get involved? Why can't you just rest in Christ's protection?

God protects us active-duty Christians from demonic influences when we take up the weapons He has designed for us according to the strategy which He has outlined

Dressed for Success

The armor God has provided for us and instructed us to wear is our main protection from the enemy.

- Look again at Ephesians 6:14-17. What does the active-duty believer wear for protection?

- According to Romans 13:12-14, what are we doing when we put on the armor of God?

When we put on Christ we put ourselves under His protection, where the evil one cannot touch us (1 John 5:18).

Armor You Have Already Put On

- Explain in your own words the importance of the following three pieces of armor—pieces which you were given when you first received Jesus Christ. How does each piece help you in battle? What are you doing to stand firm in each of them? Be specific.

  — The belt of truth

  — The breastplate of righteousness

— The shoes of peace

We stand firm in the truth by relating everything we do to the truth of God's Word. We stand firm in righteousness when we confess our sins and agree with God about where we fall short. And we stand firm in peace when we fill our heart with God's Word and act as peacemakers in our relationships.

The Rest of the Wardrobe

- Now explain in your own words the importance of each of the following three pieces of armor, pieces which you yourself must put on to protect yourself from Satan's attack. How does each of these help you in battle? What are you doing to put them to use? Be specific.

  — The shield of faith

  — The helmet of salvation

  — The sword of the Spirit

The more you know about God and His Word, the greater your shield. And no matter what the outcome of your daily spiritual battles, the helmet of salvation guarantees your eternal victory. Finally, be bold in speaking aloud God's powerful truth.

The Protective Power of Prayer

We never know completely the effects of our prayers. But we do know that God includes our prayer as part of His strategy for establishing His kingdom.

- When have you been most aware that, in Mary's words, "Prayer works!... Prayer is powerful!"?

- Read Ephesians 6:18, the command which follows the description of the armor God has provided for us.

  — Neil and Dave define prayer as "communication with God by which we tell Him we are depending on Him." How well does this statement describe your prayers? Are you deferring to God's wisdom or asking Him to bless your ideas and plans? Are you acknowledging God's perfect timing and ways or are you telling Him what to do?

  — As an active-duty believer, do you regularly spend time in the presence of your Commander? Do you balance your time spent speaking to Him with time spent listening for His orders?

Praying for Spiritual Sight

- We are to use prayer to combat spiritual blindness. We need to ask God's Spirit to open the eyes of people who have not yet come to Christ, and we need to ask that the eyes of believers be opened to a greater understanding of our spiritual power, authority, and protection in Christ.

— For whom can you pray that God's light would penetrate the blindness caused by Satan?

— Now write out a two- or three-sentence prayer for believers like yourself. How would you like God to improve your spiritual sight?

Our strategy for bringing others to Christ must include prayer that God's Spirit will open their spiritual eyes. We believers also need to continually pray for each other that Satan's lies will be blown away and that our vision into the spiritual world will be crystal clear.

Binding the Strong Man

• We are also to use prayer to bind the "strong man"— that is, Satan and his demons, who won't let go of things they wrongfully hold until we exercise our authority in Christ.

— What can you learn from Bill's experience (pages 91-92 of the text)?

— Where in your life or in the life of someone you know do you see evidence of the strong man's grip?

— What prayer for that situation will you begin praying today?

God has equipped you with everything you need to ward off the attack of the strong man in your life. He has also equipped and authorized you for "search and rescue" in the lives of those who are in the devil's clutches. And He has given you the armor and the weapons you need for these battles.

A Step toward Freedom

• Look again at Ephesians 6:10-18. Which of the six pieces of God's armor do you need to focus on in your spiritual conflicts at home, at school, and with friends? What will you do to prepare that piece of armor for battle? Be specific about your action plan— or talk to a pastor or youth-group leader who can give you ideas about what you could do to prepare your armor for battle.

• Spend a few moments in prayer, talking to God about each piece of armor He has given you. Ask God to give you a clearer understanding of His truth, your righteousness in Christ, and His peace so that you might stand firm in these. Ask God, too, to help you learn more about Him and His Word, trust in the salvation He has provided for you, and ably wield the sword of God's Word. Then pray for spiritual sight for those who are spiritually blind and for improved vision for those believers you know. Finally, in Christ's name, bind the strong man in whatever situations you are aware of him working his evil. Close your prayer by thanking God for the protection He has provided for the battle and asking Him to enable you to serve Him and His kingdom well.

6

Dealing with Evil in Person

The Devil and His Lies

- What did Neil learn from his encounter with the demon influencing Evelyn?

- What can you learn from this account of Evelyn and Maggie McKendall?

Jesus warned in John 8:44 that whenever Satan speaks a lie, "he speaks from his own nature; for he is a liar, and the father of lies."

A Rebel Authority Is in Control

We live in a world which is under the authority of an evil ruler, but it wasn't always that way.

- The answers to the following questions outline key events in the history of God's world.

— Why did Adam lose his authority to rule over creation?

— Satan became the rebel holder of authority. What ended his rule?

— Who now has the ultimate authority over heaven and earth? See 1 John 3:8 as well as Matthew 28:18.

The Powers That Be

• Many Christians who agree that Satan is a living being who is responsible for the evil in the world today nevertheless resist any talk about demons.

— How did you react when you first heard about demons?

— Do most of your friends believe that Satan and demons exist? What do you believe?

— What does the fact that Satan is not always present, all-knowing, or all-powerful suggest about whether demons exist and serve as his emissaries?

— What do Neil and Dave say in answer to the question, What should we do about Satan's demonic powers? Explain the reasons for their answer.

Satan and his demons need not frighten us, for—to quote the apostle John—"greater is he who is in you than he who is in the world" (1 John 4:4).

The Personality of Demons

The Bible does not attempt to prove the existence of demons any more than it attempts to prove the existence of God. It simply reports on their activities as if its readers accepted their existence—which early believers did.

- Review on pages 103–104 the text's discussion of the following eight insights (gleaned from Luke 11:24-26) into the personality and individuality of evil spirits. Then answer the questions which follow.

    1. Demons can exist outside or inside humans.

    2. Demons are unable to travel at will.

    3. Demons are able to communicate.

    4. Each demon has a separate identity.

    5. Demons are able to remember and make plans.

6. Demons are able to evaluate and make decisions.

7. Demons are able to combine forces.

8. Demons vary in degrees of wickedness.

— Which of these characteristics of demons were new to you?

— How does this list affect your perspective on demons? Do they seem more or less frightening? Why?

• Turn to Ephesians 6:10. How are we to respond to Satan's attacks?

Consciously place yourself in the Lord's hands and resist Satan and his demons by speaking aloud God's Word. You are only open to the devil's arrows when you are walking by sight instead of by faith or walking in the flesh instead of in the Spirit.

Dealing with the Evil Around Us

Your Christian life is the process of walking toward Jesus Christ down a long street lined on both sides with two-story houses. There is absolutely nothing in the street that can keep you from reaching Jesus. But since this world is under the control of Satan, those houses are filled with beings committed to keeping you from reaching Jesus. What are they calling out to you?

- "Hey, look over here! I have something you really want. It tastes good, feels good, and is a lot more fun than your boring walk down the street. Come on in and take a look."

  — What temptations are you most vulnerable to?

  — Read Matthew 4:1-11. Why was Jesus able to stand strong against Satan?

  — Like Jesus, you need to turn to God's Word for strength in the face of temptation. For each of the specific temptations you listed above, write out a verse that will help you resist it.

- "You're stupid. You're ugly. You'll never amount to anything for God" and, "See what you did! How can you call yourself a Christian when you behave like that?"

  — What accusations do you battle most often?

— How do those accusations affect your Christian walk?

— Write out a specific verse from God's Word as a response to each of the accusations you listed above.

• "You don't need to go to youth group today. It's not important to pray and read the Bible every day. Some of the New Age stuff isn't so bad."

— What aspects of your Christian walk does Satan try to discourage with his sly words of deception, ideas which he often introduces with "I" and therefore sound like thoughts that were yours instead of his?

— What commands or encouragements from the Bible can help you continue walking the walk you're called to?

• Having looked more closely at how Satan works, do you think a Christian needs to know the Bible? Why or why not?

Satan will indeed try to tempt, accuse, deceive, and control you, but remember that he has absolutely no power or authority to keep you from steadily moving forward in your walk toward Christ. He can never again own you because you have been redeemed by Jesus Christ and you are forever in Him (1 Peter 1:18,19).

Levels of Bondage

If you allow Satan to influence you long enough through temptation, accusation, and deception, he can gradually come to control you. We'll look at three levels of spiritual conflict, which involve 85 percent of today's Christian young people.

- Neil and Dave estimate that about 65 percent of all Christians are living at the first level of spiritual conflict but don't recognize it as a spiritual conflict. What characterizes this level?

- What characterizes the second level of conflict—a level experienced by about 15 percent of all Christians?

- Sadly, about 5 percent of the Christian community falls victim to the third level of spiritual conflict. What do these people experience?

- Why do you think no more than 15 percent of all Christian young people are completely free of Satan's bondage?

- What are you doing to avoid Satan's bondage so that you can walk according to the Spirit and bear fruit for God's kingdom?

Our level of bondage is the result of how we respond to the temptations, accusations, and deceptions that demons throw our way. Are you responding correctly?

Just Say No

There are three ways to respond to the demons' fiery arrows, and two of these ways are wrong. Review pages 108-109 of the text.

- Which two responses to Satan are wrong and worthless?

- What is the correct response to Satan's temptations, accusations, and deceptions?

- What practical command in 2 Corinthians 10:5b can keep you walking the road toward Christ?

As you travel on your journey toward Christ, raise your shield of faith whenever Satan sends temptations, accusations, and deceptions your way. Take every thought captive to the obedience of Christ. Choose truth in the face of every lie. As you do, you'll find your faith deepening and your freedom increasing with every step.

A Step toward Freedom

- What, if anything, did you find disturbing in this chapter? Turn to your Bible for answers and don't hesitate to share your concerns with your pastor.

- What statements in this chapter were especially encouraging? Make a note of those statements and of verses like Ephesians 6:10, which will help provide the strength and courage you need to continue your walk of faith.

- Thank God, your almighty heavenly Father, for the protection He gives you and the authority you have in Christ to stand strong against Satan and his demons. Confess any fear you have about evil spirits or Satan and ask God to give you confidence and peace in Him. Finally, pray out loud—today and every day—"By the power and the blood of the Lord Jesus Christ, I command any and all evil to leave my presence."

7
The Lure of Knowledge and Power

A Deal with the Devil

• What did you learn from Neil's account of Harry's bondage to Satan?

• What is one reason Satan often chooses to display his power? How do such displays contribute to his efforts to deceive?

• What did you learn from the way Neil handled himself in the face of Satan's fearsome display of power?

• How is leaving behind one's involvement in Satanism like leaving behind alcoholism?

The apostle Peter instructs us as believers to resist the
devil and stand firm in our faith (1 Peter 5:9). When we
stand up to Satan, he has no choice but to eventually
back down, as he did when Neil met with Harry.

A Trap as Old as the Bible

How do people like Harry get trapped in the quicksand
of Satan's control in the first place? One of Satan's major
traps is his appeal to the human desire for spiritual
knowledge and power.

• Our desire for knowledge and power is God-given.

— With what are we supposed to fulfill that desire
   for knowledge and power?

— What does Satan the deceiver offer us?

— Explain how the sin of divination or witchcraft is a
   form of rebellion against God.

• When 1292 high-school students were surveyed,
  approximately one-third admitted that they had been

involved in spiritual practices God clearly says are wrong.

— In Deuteronomy 18:9-13, what practices does God forbid?

— Which of these do you see being done today?

— What are your thoughts about horoscopes? How involved have you been in astrology? Have you read your horoscope for guidance? For entertainment? Or not at all?

Many of the high-school students surveyed argued that their horoscopes worked most of the time, but that is not the point. The issue is that God says it isn't right for His people to be turning to astrology.

• Police departments are trying to let the public know that Satanism is a very real problem in today's society.

— Are you aware of Satanism on your campus?

— What kind of New Age teachings or practices do you see in your school?

— What do you think is the appeal of Satanism to your peers?

Every unthinkable act that Moses warned Israel not to get involved in—from horoscopes to animal and human sacrifices—is in place and operating in our culture today. And they all have their root in Satan's deception.

Knowledge from the Dark Side

Many people today are craving knowledge about life, but they don't want to hear what God has to say.

- What warning does God give us in Leviticus 19:31; 20:6,27 (quoted on pages 116-117 of the text)?

- Why do you think words from a psychic or a channeler are more appealing to people than what God has to say?

- What do you think Satan is doing through today's psychics, palm-readers, card-readers, and other New Age practitioners? What is Satan's ultimate goal?

Mediums: Phony and for Real

- What is the source of information for phony mediums? For real mediums?

The Down Side of Seeking the Dark Side

- Let's look again at the account of Saul, Israel's first king. We learn that "the Spirit of the LORD departed from Saul, and an evil spirit from the LORD terrorized him" (1 Samuel 16:14).

  — First, explain in your own words how the relationship between God's Spirit and the Old Testament king Saul is different from the relationship between God's Spirit and New Testament believers today.

  — Second, why would God send an evil spirit to a person or a nation?

  — What does 1 Corinthians 5:5 say in response to the preceding question?

  — Finally, what did you learn about music in this discussion of "the down side of seeking the dark side"?

God clearly forbids communicating with the dead (Isaiah 8:19,20), and in the story of the rich man and Lazarus, Jesus teaches the present-day impossibility of communicating with the dead (Luke 16:19-31). So remember that when the media heralds psychics who claim to have contacted the dead and New Age mediums who report to have channeled a person from the past into the present, such actions are nothing more than the activities of a demon or the tricks of a con artist.

An Old Idea in New Clothing

• The thirst for knowledge and power has lured many young people to seek guidance from mediums and spiritists and from such occultic practices as fortune-telling, tarot cards, palm-reading, Ouija boards, astrology, magic charming, and automatic writing.

— What are you doing to satisfy your thirst for knowledge and power? To whom or what are you turning?

— What would you say to a friend who is dabbling in fortune-telling, tarot cards, palm-reading, Ouija boards, or astrology—or is thinking about doing so?

— What are you doing to avoid being drawn into New Age thinking?

God promises to love and guide you. Know that you can indeed find the knowledge you desire in Him.

A Step toward Freedom

- The account of Saul may have raised some questions in your mind about your own salvation. Know that, as a New Testament believer, your situation is quite different from Saul's. Consider the promises God has made to you in Ephesians 1:13,14; John 10:28; and Romans 8:35-39. Sum them up below and choose one of the passages to memorize.

- God will indeed enable you to stand strong against the lure of satanic knowledge. Your knowledge of His Word is key, but prayer is also essential. So ask God now to begin cutting off any craving you might have for hidden knowledge or power. Ask Him to also show you the practices you have been involved in which He forbids so that you can confess and renounce them. Finally, thank God for the hope and strength that come from knowing that nothing will ever separate you from His love.

8
Enticed to Do It Your Way

An Invitation to Refuse

• Dave remembers very vividly an early experience with temptation. What is your earliest memory of being tempted to do something you knew wasn't right? Did you say yes or no to the temptation? What lesson did you learn from the experience?

• What was your most recent experience with temptation? Did you say yes to the temptation? Why or why not?

It's important to be able to recognize temptation right away and quickly refuse Satan's invitation to do things your way. That's what we'll work on here.

What Is Temptation?

Temptation means being enticed to have your needs met through the world, the flesh, and the devil instead of through Christ (Philippians 4:19).

- Every temptation is an invitation to do things our way instead of God's way.

  — Does this definition work for you? Do you find that the temptations you face are invitations to do things your way instead of God's way? Give a specific example or two.

  — Review the list on pages 127-128 of the text. In any of these areas, we are tempted to take the good things that God created and take them beyond the boundary of His will. Which good things are you at risk of pushing beyond God's will? What warnings do you find addressed to you in this list?

- Explain the difference between sin and temptation. Feel free to talk in terms of windows and doors, as Neil and Dave did.

- Now explain the statement, "God's boundaries are not restrictive; they are protective."

God sets boundaries for us for our own good, but those boundaries don't restrict our decisions or our actions. We are free to choose whether or not to respect God's guidelines and experience the protection they offer.

Channels of Temptation

You will be better prepared to resist temptation when you realize that, according to 1 John 2:15-17 and elsewhere in the Scriptures, there are only three channels through which Satan will entice you to act outside of God's will. And Jesus models for us how we can conquer every temptation Satan throws at us.

The Lust of the Flesh

- The lust of the flesh tempts us to fulfill our physical appetites (food, sex, comfort, and so on) in a sinful, worldly way.

  — What can you learn from the discussion of Adam and Eve about how Satan uses this channel of temptation—our physical appetites—in our lives?

  — What can you learn from Jesus' temptation in the wilderness about how we can stand strong against the lust of the flesh?

  — Satan learned that Jesus was hungry by watching Him go without food for 40 days. What are some common ways that Satan and his demons try to tempt us in connection with our physical appetites?

— What specific invitations is Satan extending to you to meet your physical needs in ways that are outside the boundaries of God's will?

The temptation of the lust of the flesh is designed to draw us away from the will of God to please ourselves (Galatians 5:16,17). When you resist these temptations, you are declaring your dependence on God for your natural needs.

The Lust of the Eyes

- The lust of the eyes tempts us to do what we think is best instead of obeying the Bible.

  — What can you learn from the discussion of Adam and Eve about how Satan uses this channel of temptation—the lust of the eyes—in our lives?

  — What can you learn from Jesus' temptation in the wilderness about how we can stand strong against the lust of the eyes?

— What are some common ways that we are tempted to trust in ourselves and our own knowledge rather than in God and His Word? Asked differently, what things in the world can tempt you to stray from making your relationship with God and pleasing Him your top priority?

— In what areas of your life, if any, have you adopted a "prove it to me" attitude toward God and His commands and promises?

The lust of the eyes gradually draws us away from the Word of God and eats away at our confidence in Him. We see what the world has to offer and we desire those things more than our relationship with God. When you resist the temptations of the lust of the eyes, you are choosing to follow the Word of God instead of your own idea of how to run your life.

The Pride of Life

• The pride of life tempts us to gain attention and glory for ourselves. This channel of temptation is at the heart of the New Age movement: the temptation to direct our future, rule our world, and be our own god.

— What can you learn from the discussion of Adam and Eve about how Satan uses this channel of temptation—the pride of life—in our lives?

— What can you learn from Jesus' temptation in the wilderness about how we can stand strong against the pride of life?

— When have you felt that you don't need God's help or direction? Looking back, do you see how Satan worked to bring about that feeling?

— When have you learned the hard way—by giving in to this temptation—that the things of the world don't satisfy?

The temptation of the pride of life is intended to steer us away from the worship of God and destroy our obedience to Him by urging us to take charge of our own lives. And when you take charge of your own life, you may think you are serving yourself, but you are really worshiping and serving Satan—which is what he wants more than anything else.

• Three critical issues are reflected in these channels of temptation we've looked at:

  1. The will of God in your life, as seen in your dependence on God.

  2. The Word of God in your life, as seen in your confidence in God.

3. The worship of God in your life, as seen in
   your obedience to God.

— What does this three-part lens help you understand about the temptations you face?

— What does this three-panel mirror help you realize
about yourself and the current state of your relationship with the Lord?

The devil's hook is his deception that what we think we
want and need outside God's will can satisfy us. But only
right relationships, living by the power of the Holy
Spirit, and experiencing the fruit of the Spirit will satisfy
us.

The Way of Escape

Satan is clever in his deceit and sly in his ways, but he
need not win in our lives.

• What good news does 1 Corinthians 10:13 have for
  you?

The escape hatch that Paul talks about in 1 Corinthians
10:13 is right where temptations start—in your mind.
That is why Paul instructs us to take every thought
captive to the obedience of Christ (2 Corinthians 10:5).
The key to resisting temptation is to capture every
thought as soon as it enters your mind.

- When you capture a thought, you then need to see if it passes the eight-part test for what you should think about—a test based on Philippians 4:8.

  1. Does this thought line up with God's truth?

  2. Does it suggest that I do something honorable?

  3. Is it right?

  4. Is it pure?

  5. Will the outcome of this thought be lovely?

  6. Will the result be something to admire?

  7. Will it contribute to excellence in my life?

  8. Is it something for which I can praise God?

— Think back on a time when you failed to resist temptation. Which question(s) might have helped you recognize the temptation right when the idea entered your mind?

— Perhaps you are wrestling with a temptation right now. Ask these questions of the idea you are considering. If the answer to any of these questions is no, what are you to do with the thought?

When you learn to respond to tempting thoughts by stopping them right when they enter your mind, evaluating them on the basis of God's Word, and dismissing those which fail the test of Philippians 4:8, you have found the way of escape that God's Word promises.

Confess and Resist

- Some Christians complain about being caught in the sin-confess cycle, and you may be one of them. If so, you know how easy it is to lose hope that you can experience any real victory over sin.

  — Explain how, in the sin-confess-sin-confess cycle, Satan the tempter becomes Satan the accuser.

  — The step which breaks the sin-confess cycle is resisting Satan. What does James 4:7 promise about the effectiveness of this step?

When we sin, we are to confess our sin. Then we are to turn to Jesus Christ, our righteous defender. In His power, we will be able to stand strong the next time Satan tempts us. We will be able to experience victory and freedom over temptation and sin.

A Step toward Freedom

- Write Philippians 4:8 on an index card and memorize it. Let it stand at the doorway of your mind as a guard that evaluates every thought that wants to enter.

- Thank God for what you've learned in this chapter about temptation and sin . . . for the clear picture you have of the three channels Satan uses and the three critical issues which arise with such temptations . . . and for the promises of 1 Corinthians 10:13 and James 4:7. Then lay before God an area of temptation you're struggling with in your life. Ask Him to give you the strength you need to stand strong.

9

Don't Believe Everything You Hear

Crippling Accusations

- Remember Dave's experience before the championship wrestling match? When have your thoughts ("I'm not good enough," "I can't do it") been the reason for your defeat?

- Why is it safe to say that such discouraging inner criticism may have its roots in the kingdom of darkness? Why would Satan want this weapon in his arsenal?

- Why is it sometimes hard to ignore Satan's accusations?

• What accusations does Satan frequently use against you? Write out a verse from Scripture to counter each one of the lies you list here.

Satan can do nothing to change our position in Christ and our worth to God. But he can defeat us if he can trick us into believing his lie that we are of little value to God or other people.

Putting the Accuser in His Place

The good news is that we don't have to listen to Satan's accusations and live in defeat. Zechariah 3:1-10 shows how God responds to our accuser and teaches us an important truth about how we can stand strong against him.

The Lord Rebukes Satan

• The scene in Zechariah is a heavenly courtroom. The accused defendant is Joshua the high priest, and he represents all of God's people, including you.

— In this scene, what is Satan doing?

— What does God say in response to Satan's accusations?

While Satan accuses us before God, he and his demons also accuse us by bombarding our minds with false thoughts of how unworthy and unrighteous we are in God's sight.

> — In rebuking the accuser, God seems to say, "You're not the judge, and you cannot pass sentence on My people." Write out, in your own words, a response to Satan's accusations based on this model—and be ready to use it the next time you find yourself bombarded by thoughts of how unworthy you are.

Satan is not your judge; he is only your accuser. Don't listen to his false accusations. Listen instead to God's truth that you are right with God and, in Jesus Christ, pure and worthy and capable.

The Lord Removes Our Filthy Garments

- The reason Satan's accusations are false is because God has solved the problem of our sin, represented in Zechariah as Joshua's filthy garments.

> — Why are Satan's accusations groundless? What happened when Christ died on the cross?

> — Who removes our unrighteousness?

— Why is it good news that God changes your wardrobe and that the change is nothing you have to do for yourself?

— Why do we sometimes try to earn God's love and acceptance even though we know the Bible teaches that we already have it? Asked more personally, why do you sometimes try to earn God's love and acceptance even though the Bible teaches that you already have it?

When we give our lives to God in faith, He changes our filthy rags into new garments that are as white as snow. In Christ, God makes us clean and pure.

The Lord Asks Us to Respond

• Having rebuked Satan and provided our righteousness, the Lord calls us to respond with obedience.

— God rebukes Satan and clothes us in righteousness. According to the first part of Zechariah 3:7, what does God want us to do in response?

— What are some specific practical ways that, each day, you can walk in God's ways, serve Him, and live out your identity in Christ?

If we walk in obedience, God promises that we will share in His authority in the spiritual world and be able to live victoriously over Satan and sin. As we operate in His authority and live in fellowship with Him, our daily victory and fruitfulness are assured.

What's the Difference?

At this point, it's important to point out the difference between the devil's accusations and the Holy Spirit's convictions.

- The devil's accusations and the Holy Spirit's convictions both cause sorrow, but that sorrow moves us in two different directions.

  — Where do Satan's accusations lead? Remember Judas in Luke 22:3-5.

  — Where do the Holy Spirit's convictions lead? Think about Peter (see Luke 2:33,34 and John 21:15-17).

- How can you determine whether you are being falsely accused? The following two questions give you a good guideline.

  — What feelings and thoughts about yourself will you have if Satan is the one causing the sorrow?

— What feelings, thoughts about yourself, and actions will result if you are being convicted by the Spirit?

Satan's continuing work is to accuse God's children (Revelation 12:10), but Christ's continuing work is to pray for us (Hebrews 7:25). We have a persistent enemy, but we have an even more persistent Savior.

The Quicksand of Accusation

- It is very important to learn to resist the accusations of Satan. He never gives up. If we fail to keep resisting him, we may become targets for even more serious attacks.

  — What can you learn from the story about Janelle?

  — When have you believed Satan's lies about your worth and, as a result, walked away from God and into sin? Be specific. What did this experience teach you?

- Satan will tell believers lies about their worth. We are to ignore those lies and instead believe what God says about us. What does God say about you in the following passages?

— Romans 5:8

— 1 John 3:1

— Psalm 139

— 1 John 1:9

— Romans 8:38,39

Know that Satan the accuser is on the prowl and don't believe everything you hear. Instead, put your feelings to the test. Take every thought captive. And cling to what God says about you: It's the truth which will set you free.

A Step toward Freedom

• Read 2 Corinthians 7:9,10. Then describe a time when your loving Father did indeed bring you to a point of repentance. What did you learn from that experience? How did it help you grow closer to God?

• Thank God for His Spirit and the conviction He brings which leads to repentance and life...and thank Him that He opened the door to your eternal life through the death of His Son. Ask God to help you stand strong in the truth about who you are in

Christ and how much God loves you when Satan hurls his accusations your way. Finally, spend a few moments praising God that Satan isn't able to bring any charges against you that the blood of Christ won't cover...and that nothing can ever separate you from His love.

10

Appearances Can Be Deceiving

New Testament Hope

- To become free of the bondage of Satan's lies, Alyce needed to learn about her identity in Christ. What does the phrase "Christ in you and you in Christ" mean to you? What does this good news say about your identity?

- Satan will try to steer you away from God's truth and deceive you into believing his lies through self-deception, false prophets and teachers, and deceiving spirits. To protect yourself, what pieces of spiritual armor need to be ready for battle? See Ephesians 6:10-18.

We are easy targets for Satan's deception if we fail to fill our minds with the truth of God's Word.

Beware of Self-Deception

The Bible warns us of several ways we can deceive ourselves. So be aware!

- We deceive ourselves when we hear the Word but don't do it.

  — What does God command in James 1:22 and 2:14-20?

  — What gets in the way of you applying to your own life what you hear taught from God's Word?

- We deceive ourselves when we say we have no sin.

  — What do Romans 3:23 and 1 John 1:8 teach about sinfulness?

  — Why is it important to confess and deal with sin on a daily basis? (Remember the earthquakes!)

  — What keeps you from confessing your sin?

- We deceive ourselves when we think we are better than we are.

— What cautions do you find in Romans 12:3 and Galatians 6:3?

— Who is the source of all your goodness—your talents, your gifts, your life?

— How can you live so that God receives the credit for any good in your life?

• We deceive ourselves when we think we are smarter than we are.

— What do the following verses teach about wisdom?

1 Corinthians 3:18,19

Proverbs 3:5,6

1 Corinthians 2:16

— Why does thinking we are too smart to be vulnerable to Satan make us even more vulnerable to that sly deceiver?

- We deceive ourselves when we think we are good Christians but do not control our speech (James 1:26).

  — What does James 3:5-12 say about the power of the tongue? Note especially verse 5.

  — What could you be doing to prevent forest fires?

- We deceive ourselves when we think our sin will not lead to consequences.

  — According to Galatians 6:7-10, what can result from the seeds we sow in this life?

  — God forgives our sins, but He doesn't necessarily spare us from the consequences of those sinful acts. When did God teach you this lesson? Be specific.

- We deceive ourselves when we think people living totally in sin are Christians.

  — What does 1 Corinthians 6:9,10 teach about the importance of how we live? What does James 2:14-19,22,26 say?

— Where does your life need to match up better with what you believe?

• We deceive ourselves when we think we can always hang out with bad people and not be influenced by them.

— What do Proverbs 22:24,25 and 1 Corinthians 15:33 teach about the importance of the company we keep?

— Take a look at the people you hang out with. Who could influence you with their different values and draw you away from the Lord? What are you going to do about those relationships?

• Review again the list of self-deceptions. Which do you struggle with most?

As you can see, it is very possible for us Christians to deceive ourselves. But being aware of the false thinking you can fall into may keep that from happening to you.

Beware of False Prophets and Teachers

Scripture requires that all spiritual gifts be tested. False prophets and teachers are popular today because we Christians don't test them.

Comparing the Phony with the Real

- In Jeremiah 23, the Lord reveals several qualifications for a true prophet from God.

    A true prophet brings people to God and His Word (verses 16,21,22).

    A true prophet's dreams agree with God's Word (verses 25,28).

    A true prophet's message moves people to repent and get right with God, and does not leave them comfortable in their sin (verse 29 and 1 Peter 4:17).

    A true prophet gets his message from God, not from other people (verses 30,31).

— What can you learn about true prophets of God from this list of qualifications?

— Why is it important for Christian leaders to be accountable to other leaders?

Signs and Wonders: Who's Being Tested?

- God can still use signs and wonders to show that His Word is true, but Satan can also perform signs and wonders. He does so, however, to direct our worship away from God to himself.

— What does Deuteronomy 18:22 add to your understanding of false signs and wonders?

— An occurrence of the miraculous does not necessarily mean the presence of God. What can a
   believer do to test signs and wonders?

Counterfeits in the Church

• False prophets and false teachers are not just Eastern
  mystics and gurus and non-Christian cult leaders, as
  the apostle Peter warned in 2 Peter 2:1. Some false
  prophets and teachers are in our churches right now,
  disguised as Christian leaders.

— According to 2 Peter 2:10, what are two ways we
   can identify false prophets and teachers in the
   church?

— Are the Christian leaders whose teachings you
   listen to living a life consistent with their pro-
   fessed faith? Are these teachers accountable to
   other, more mature believers? What does a "no"
   answer to either of these questions suggest you
   do?

- Why is understanding God's Word important when it comes to spotting a false prophet?

Again, God's Word calls us to test the spirits behind the teaching we hear to be sure that we are indeed learning His truth.

Beware of Deceiving Spirits

In addition to warning us against self-deception and false prophets and teachers, the Bible warns us against the deception which comes through demonic influence.

- Dave told about Ashley, whom he'd met at a junior-high camp.

  — What did Ashley learn from Luke 16:19-26, especially verse 26?

  — What did you learn about Satan's strategies from Ashley's experience?

- Look again at page 164 in the text and the kind of prayer we need to pray in order to keep ourselves from deceiving spirits. In a few quiet moments of prayer now, let these words be your own. Ask God to open your eyes to any deception you may have accepted as truth.

Discerning Deception

Our first line of defense against Satan's deception is discernment—the act of judging whether something is right or wrong so that the right can be accepted and the wrong discarded.

- Discernment is the buzzer that sounds inside you warning that something is wrong. And discernment is an act of the Holy Spirit, who dwells within us.

   — Why is discernment an important gift to individual believers and to the church in general?

   — When has the Holy Spirit helped you recognize wrong and resist or discard it? Be specific.

- Why are we more vulnerable to Satan's deception than to his temptations or accusations?

- What is the only effective weapon against the darkness of Satan's deception? See John 8:31,32 and John 17:17.

The light of God's truth, as revealed in His Word, is the only effective weapon against the darkness of deception. Know His Word so that you can wield it effectively against the deceiver.

A Step toward Freedom

- This chapter may have given you a greater appreciation for the value of Bible study. What step will you take to strengthen your Bible study program so that you can be better equipped to see through Satan's deceptions? Be specific in your plan and realistic in your goals. It's always a good idea to have someone hold you accountable—and it's ideal to work with a partner.

- Thank God for the protection and wisdom available to you as His child. Thank Him, too, for His Spirit, who dwells within you and gives you the gift of discernment. Then ask the Holy Spirit to help you as you consider each of the areas of self-deception which Satan can use to his advantage and your disadvantage. Ask God's Spirit to help you discern where you may be deceiving yourself . . . and ask the Spirit to help you recognize any false teachers you may be influenced by . . . as well as any deceiving spirits at work in your life. Finally, thank God for His Word and ask Him to be with you as you seek to know Him better through the Scriptures.

11
The Danger of Losing Control

Satan's Control

• What did you learn about how Satan works from Sheila's experience?

• According to 1 Peter 1:17-19 and Romans 8:35-39, why does demonic bondage never mean satanic owner-ship?

Although it may not be easy to admit, we Christians can lose our freedom and can surrender to demonic influences. There is much clear evidence in Scripture that believers who repeatedly give in to temptation, accusation, and deception can fall into bondage to sin.

Demonic Control of the Saints

Since we live in a world whose god is Satan, the possibility of being tempted, deceived, and accused is con-
stant. If we allow Satan's schemes to influence us, we can
lose control to the level that we have been deceived.

- It is important to understand that Christians are targets for demonic influence.

  — What two options are we left with if we don't
    acknowledge the very real activity of demons in
    this world?

  — What thinking do these two options lead to? In
    other words, what are the consequences of blam-
    ing ourselves for the problems we face? Of blaming
    God?

We are in a winnable war against demonic powers. But,
as we've said again and again, if Satan can get you to
believe a lie, he can control your life.

- The New Testament offers examples as well as teachings that reflect the truth that believers can come
  under bondage to demonic influence.

  — *Luke 13:10-17.* Where was the woman Jesus healed
    (verse 10)? How was she described (verse 16)?
    What things didn't protect her from Satan's
    power?

— *Luke 22:31-34.* What request did Satan make of Jesus? And what does the fact that this request was made suggest about a believer's vulnerability?

— *Ephesians 6:10-17.* What does the existence of the armor Paul describes here and the command to put it on suggest about the power and strategy of demons? About your vulnerability?

— *James 3:14-16.* What does James warn believers about here?

— *1 Timothy 4:1-3.* Who will be "paying attention to deceitful spirits and doctrines of demons"? What warning is implied in this statement?

— *1 Corinthians 5:1-13.* Paul hoped that the man referred to in this passage would experience the natural consequences of his sin, repent, and be set free from his bondage. What clue in this passage suggests that the man was a believer? When have the natural consequences of your sin moved you to repent?

— *Ephesians 4:26,27.* According to this passage, what is one way we believers can give Satan a foothold in our lives? Are you nursing any anger, bitterness, or unforgiveness? If so, Satan has a place in your life from which to work.

— *1 Peter 5:6-9.* What are two more ways that we believers can give Satan a foothold in our life? Also, notice how Peter talks about the devil here. What does the image suggest to you?

— *Acts 5:1-11.* What does the story of Ananias and Sapphira teach you about the importance of truth? What does their story teach about the possibility and consequences of Satan's control of believers?

It is possible for believers—for you and for me—to be filled either with satanic deception or the Spirit of God. To whichever source we yield, by that source we shall be filled and controlled.

Responsibility for Resisting Control

When, like Ananias and Sapphira, you open the door of your life to Satan, he will take full advantage of the opportunity.

• Consider again the story of Ananias and Sapphira.

— Read Peter's questions to them in Acts 5:4,9. What do you think prompted them to lie about the income they received from the sale of their land?

— What is inaccurate about the statement, "The devil made me do it"? How is a person's freedom to make choices involved in the devil's control of his or her life?

When we fail to resist temptation, accusation, or deception, Satan will enter our life. If we continue to allow him access to that area, he will eventually control it. We won't lose our salvation, but we will lose our daily victory.

— Despite this truth, many young Christians who cannot control some area of their life blame themselves instead of dealing with the problem. How might Satan be involved in this?

— An area of bondage is anything bad you cannot stop doing and anything good you cannot make yourself do. According to this definition, what areas of bondage—if any—exist in your life today? If there are any areas, what will you do to resist Satan? Who will you go to for support?

We have all the resources and protection we need to live a victorious life in Christ every day. If we're not living it, it's our choice.

If We're Not Responsible, We Will Lose Control

- God's protection depends on our willingness to apply the protection He has provided.

  — According to the following passages, what must you do to experience God's protection?

  Romans 13:14

  James 4:7

  Ephesians 6:10-17

  Romans 6:12

Choosing truth, living a righteous life, and putting on the armor of God is each believer's individual responsibility. If you go into battle without your armor, you may get hurt—and you alone are responsible for putting on that armor. You alone make such choices for yourself, choices to protect yourself from Satan by not giving him a foothold in your life.

A Step toward Freedom

- Read what Paul says in Romans 7:15. What about yourself—if anything—do his words remind you of?

If you yourself could have written these words today, let the prayer below guide you through a time of confession. If you aren't struggling right now, thank God and ask Him to protect you from being proud of that fact, for pride can serve as a foothold for Satan.

• Knowing that the apostle Paul himself struggled with doing the very thing he hated, confess to God where you have been doing exactly what you hate . . . confess where you now see that you were a target for Satan's temptation, accusation, and deception. If you're not sure, ask God to help you see yourself as He sees you: as you really are. Having recognized Satan's activity in your life, now confess how you gave him a foothold in your life . . . and renounce your involvement with him. Finally, thank God for the gift of His Son, the Bondage Breaker, and for the freedom that is available to you in Jesus Christ.

12

Steps to Freedom in Christ

Taking Inventory

If you have received Christ as your personal Savior, He has set you free from sin and Satan's power through His victory on the cross and His resurrection. But if you are not experiencing freedom in your daily life, it may be because you have not realized who you are in Christ and taken a stand against the devil and his lies.

- In what areas of your life, if any, are you not experiencing freedom?

- Have you lost a measure of your freedom in Christ because you have disobeyed Him? Confess that disobedience. Be specific.

Now you can begin working through the following seven steps toward full freedom and victory in Christ. Again, keep in mind that no one can take these steps for you.

- As you take these steps, who will be walking this path with you? Who will be praying for you? What mature Christian will be helping you and encouraging you each step of the way?

The battle for your mind can only be won as you personally choose truth—and know that you are entering a battle which, with the protection God has provided for you and in Christ, you can win.

An Opening Prayer

- As the battle unfolds, you may find yourself thinking, "This isn't going to work" or, "God doesn't love me."

— Who is the source of thoughts like these?

— What will you do to defend yourself against them?

Satan's lies can stop you only if you believe them. Uncover the lie and Satan's power is broken.

- Explain why you must speak out loud when you uncover Satan's lies and want to confront him.

- Now pray aloud the following prayer:

> Dear heavenly Father, I know that You are here in this room and present in my life. You are the only all-knowing, all-powerful, ever-present God. I desperately need You because without Jesus I can do nothing. I believe the Bible because it tells me what is really true. I refuse to believe the lies of Satan. I stand in the truth that all authority in heaven and on earth has been given to the risen Christ. I ask You to protect my thoughts and mind, to fill me with Your Holy Spirit, and to lead me into all the truth. I pray for Your complete protection. In Jesus' name I pray. Amen.

Then have your Christian friend or counselor declare aloud these truths:

> In the name and the authority of the Lord Jesus Christ, we command Satan and all evil to let go of (name) in order that (name) can be free to know and choose to do the will of God. As children of God seated with Christ in the heavenlies, we agree that every enemy of the Lord Jesus Christ be bound and gagged to silence in (name). We say to Satan and all of his evil workers that

you cannot inflict any pain or in any way stop or hinder God's will from being done today in (name).

Having commanded Satan and his evil workers to leave you alone, you can now begin working on these seven steps.

Step 1: Counterfeit Versus Real

The first step to freedom in Christ is to turn your back on any present or past involvement with satanically inspired occult practices or false religions.

• Pray aloud the following prayer:

> Dear heavenly Father, I ask You to reveal to me anything that I have done or that someone has done to me that is spiritually wrong. Show me how I have been involved with any cults, false religions, occult/satanic practices, or false teachers, whether I knew I was involved or not. I want to experience Your freedom and do Your will. I ask this in Jesus' name. Amen.

• Complete, if you haven't already, the "Non-Christian Spiritual Checklist" found on page 189 of the text.

- Now list the titles of anti-Christian movies, music, books, magazines, comic books, TV programs, video games, and anything else which may have influenced you in a wrong way.

- Answer the following six questions:

    Have you ever felt, heard, or seen a spiritual being in your room?

    Have you had an imaginary friend who talks to you?

    Have you ever heard voices in your head or had repeating, nagging thoughts like, "I'm dumb," "I'm ugly," "I can't do anything right," and so on, as if there were a conversation going on in your head?

    Have you or anyone in your family ever consulted a medium, spiritist, or channeler?

    What other spiritual experiences have you had that could be considered out of the ordinary (telepathy, speaking in a trance, knowing something supernaturally)?

    Have you ever been involved in satanic worship of any form or attended a concert where Satan was the focus?

- Then, as you were directed in the text, pray the following prayer for each item on your list:

> Lord, I confess that I have participated in
> _____. I ask Your forgiveness, and I re-
> nounce _____ as a counterfeit to true
> Christianity.

To experience true freedom in Christ, you must renounce all contact with cults, false religions, occult/satanic practices, and false teachers as the Lord allows you to remember them. You must recognize that they are counterfeits to true Christianity.

Step 2: Deception Versus Truth

Second, you must choose God's truth and get rid of anything false in your life (Ephesians 4:15,25).

• Begin this important step by reading aloud the following prayer:

> Dear heavenly Father, I know that You want me to face the truth and that I must be honest with You. I know that choosing to believe the truth will set me free (John 8:32). I have been deceived by Satan, the father of lies (John 8:44), and I have deceived myself (1 John 1:8). I thought I could hide it from You, but You see everything and still love me. I pray in the name of the Lord Jesus Christ, asking You to rebuke all of Satan's demons through Your righteous Son Jesus, who shed His blood on the cross and rose from the dead for me. I have asked Jesus into my life, and I

am Your child. Therefore, by the authority of the Lord Jesus Christ I command all evil spirits to leave me. I ask the Holy Spirit to lead me into all truth. I ask You to look deep inside me and know my heart. Show me if there is anything in me that I am trying to hide (Psalm 139:23,24), because I want to be free. In Jesus' name I pray. Amen.

• Now think about the evil tricks Satan has used to deceive you.

— Have you been listening to false teachers or deceiving spirits? Have you been living under self-deception? Have you made excuses to defend your behavior?

— Complete the inventory found on page 193 of the text.

— For each item you check on the inventory, pray this prayer:

Lord, I agree that I have been deceived in the area of _____. Thank You for forgiving me. I commit myself to know and follow Your truth.

- Choosing truth may be difficult if you have been living a lie (been deceived) for some time. Filling your mind and heart with the truth is the best way to free yourself of Satan's deception.

— Read aloud the Statement of Truth (pages 194-196).

— What questions, if any, do you have about what you've read? Get answers from a pastor, youth leader, or more mature Christian so that you can read these words of truth with conviction.

Read the Statement of Truth every day for several weeks in order to renew your mind and build your faith. After all, that's what God's truth is designed to do.

Step 3: Bitterness Versus Forgiveness

If you do not forgive people who hurt you or offend you, you are a wide-open target for Satan's attacks. You need to forgive others so that Satan can't take advantage of you (2 Corinthians 2:10,11).

- Ask God to bring to mind those people you need to forgive as you read the prayer below. Make a list of those names.

> Dear heavenly Father, thank You for Your kindness and patience which led me to turn from my sin (Romans 2:4). I have not always been kind, patient, and loving toward others, especially those who have hurt me. I have been bitter

and resentful. I give You my emotions, and ask You to bring to the surface all my painful memories so I can choose to forgive from my heart. I ask You to bring to my mind the people I need to forgive (Matthew 18:35). I ask this in the precious name of Jesus, who will heal me from my hurts. Amen.

• Did your name appear on the list? Did you list God? What do you need to forgive yourself for? What anger toward God do you need to confess?

• Now review the discussion of forgiveness (pages 198-199).

— What ideas about forgiveness are new to you?

— What encouragement did you find in this discussion? What conviction?

• Having been nudged by the Holy Spirit, choose to forgive the people on your list. Don't wait to forgive until you feel like forgiving. You'll never get there. Forgive those who have hurt you by praying aloud, "Lord, I forgive (name) for (specifically name all of his/her offenses and your painful memories)."

Remember that you forgive someone for your sake so
that you can be free. Your need to forgive isn't an issue
between you and the person who hurt you; it's between
you and God.

Step 4: Rebellion Versus Submission

The Bible teaches that we have two responsibilities to the
human authorities God has placed over us: pray for them
and submit to them. Disobeying God's commands and
rebelling against God, your parents, and other authorities gives Satan an opportunity to attack.

- Explain why being submissive to parents, teachers,
  and the government demonstrates your faith in God.

- Under what circumstances does God permit us to
  disobey earthly leaders? The Bible is very specific.

- If you have questions about how God wants you to
  respond to authorities in your life, talk to your pastor
  or youth leader or open the Bible to some of the
  passages listed on page 200 of the text.

- Now take Step 4.

  — Pray aloud the following prayer:

    Dear heavenly Father, You have said in the
    Bible that rebellion is as bad as witchcraft and

disobedience as sinful as serving false gods (1 Samuel 15:23). I know that I have disobeyed You by rebelling in my heart against You and those You have put in authority over me. I ask Your forgiveness for my rebellion. By the shed blood of the Lord Jesus Christ I resist all evil spirits who took advantage of my rebellion. I pray that You will show me all the ways I have been rebellious. I choose to adopt a submissive spirit and servant's heart. In the name of Jesus Christ my Lord. Amen.

— Ask God to forgive you for those times you have not been submissive.

— Then declare your trust that God will work through His line of authority by praying this prayer:

Lord, I agree I have been rebellious toward _____. Please forgive me for this rebellion. I choose to be submissive and obedient to Your Word. In Jesus' name. Amen.

When we submit to God's line of authority, we are choosing to believe that God will protect and bless us.

Step 5: Pride Versus Humility

Pride says, "I can do it! I can get myself out of this mess without God or anyone else's help."

- Why is pride a killer?

- Explain what is meant by the statement, "Humility is confidence properly placed."

- Now take Step 5 toward freedom.

  — Begin by expressing your commitment to live humbly before God. Let the prayer below guide you:

     Dear heavenly Father, You have said that pride goes before destruction and an arrogant spirit before stumbling (Proverbs 16:18). I confess that I have been thinking mainly of myself and not of others. I have not denied myself, picked up my cross daily, and followed You (Matthew 16:24). I have believed that I am the only one who cares about me, so I must take care of myself. I have turned away from You and have not let You love me. I am tired of living for myself and by myself. I now confess that I have sinned against You by placing my will before Yours and by centering my life around self instead of You. I renounce my pride and selfishness. I cancel any ground gained by the enemies of the Lord Jesus Christ. I ask You to fill me with Your Holy Spirit so I can do Your will. I give my heart to You and stand against all the ways that Satan attacks me. I ask You to show me how to live for others. I now choose to make others more important than myself and to make You the most important of all (Romans 12:10). I ask this in the name of Christ Jesus my Lord. Amen.

— Now allow God to show you any specific areas in your life where you have been prideful. God can use the list on page 203 to prompt you.

— For each statement on page 203 that is true for you, pray, "Lord, I agree that I have been prideful in the area of _____. Please forgive me for my pride. I choose to humble myself and place all my confidence in You. In Jesus' name. Amen."

When we are prideful, we place our will before God's and center our life on ourselves instead of God. When we humbly acknowledge who God is, we once again place Him on the throne at the center of our life.

Step 6: Bondage Versus Freedom

This step to freedom deals with sins which have become habits.

• Have any sins in your life become habits? The answer may be yes if you feel caught in the trap of sin-confess-sin-confess.

- James 5:16 tells us to confess our sin to one another. What spiritually mature person will you confess to and then ask to hold you up in prayer and check in on you from time to time?

- Rewrite the promise of 1 John 1:9, using the words "I," "my," and "me." After all, this promise is for you!

- Now work through the elements of Step 6.

  — Whether you need to confess to others or just to God, pray the prayer below:

    Dear heavenly Father, You have said, "Put on the Lord Jesus Christ, and make no provision for the flesh in regard to its lusts" (Romans 13:14). I understand that I have given in to fleshly lusts which wage war against my soul (1 Peter 2:11). I thank You that in Christ my sins are forgiven, but I have broken Your holy law and given the enemy an opportunity to wage war in my body (Romans 6:12,13; James 4:1; 1 Peter 5:8). I come before Your presence to admit these sins and to seek Your cleansing (1 John 1:9) that I may be freed from the bondage of sin. I now ask You to reveal to my mind the ways that I have broken Your moral law and disappointed the Holy Spirit. In Jesus' precious name I pray. Amen.

— Now, referring to the section "Special Prayers for Specific Needs," pray those prayers which apply to you. You'll find prayers for sins of the flesh, homosexuality, abortion, suicidal tendencies, eating disorders, cutting on yourself, and substance abuse.

— After you have confessed all the sin you are aware of, close with this prayer:

Dear Father, I now confess these sins to You and claim, through the blood of the Lord Jesus Christ, my forgiveness and cleansing. I cancel all ground that evil spirits have gained through my willful involvement in sin. I ask this in the wonderful name of my Lord and Savior Jesus Christ. Amen.

When you confess your sin, God washes you whiter than snow. In His power, you can be free from the bondage of sin. In His strength, you can walk according to His laws and commands.

Step 7: Curses Versus Blessing

The last step to freedom is to turn your back on the sins of your ancestors (parents, grandparents, great-grandparents, and so on) and any curses which may have been placed on you.

• Evil spirits can be passed down to us from sinful members of the previous generations. The actions of our ancestors may have given Satan a foothold in our families.

— As far as you know, have any of your ancestors done anything that might have given Satan a foothold in the family?

— In order to walk free from past influences, make the declaration found on pages 209-210 of the text.

— Follow up your declaration with prayer. This model may help:

Dear heavenly Father, I come to You as Your child, purchased by the blood of the Lord Jesus Christ. You are the Lord of the universe and the Lord of my life. I submit my body to You as an instrument of righteousness, a living sacrifice, that I may glorify You in my body. I now ask You to fill me with Your Holy Spirit. I commit myself to the renewing of my mind in order to prove that Your will is good, perfect, and acceptable for me (Romans 12:2). All this I do in the name and authority of the Lord Jesus Christ. Amen.

- Once you have secured your freedom by going through these seven steps, you may find demonic influences attempting reentry days or even months later.

  — Why would Satan's demons not give up easily?

  — What will you do to remain in right relationship with God and free of Satan's hold? Be specific.

When we call upon Jesus, the highest authority in heaven and earth, He escorts the enemy out of our lives. But it's our responsibility not to let him back in. We must know the truth, stand firm, and resist the evil one.

A Step toward Freedom

- Read Galatians 5:1. What does this promise mean to you personally? Memorize this verse and cling to its truth whenever Satan's demons attempt to enter or reenter your life.

- As you pray, thank God for the freedom available in Him. Thank Him, too, for His love for you, a love which will never let you go. Then ask your all-knowing and almighty Father to show you what in your life may be keeping you from living free in Christ . . . and to give you the strength you need as you battle Satan and his demons. Close with a prayer of commitment. Let God know of your determination to continue to grow in Him and walk in the freedom He offers you.

13

Living Free and Staying Free

The freedom you gained by working through the steps to freedom in Chapter 12 must be maintained. You have won a very important battle, but the war goes on. So now we'll look at six important Bible-based guidelines to help you maintain your freedom and walk in Christ.

Remember that you don't get any extra points with God if you follow these six guidelines. Neither do you lose points with Him if you ignore them. God loves you whether you follow His guidelines or not. However, His strong desire is that you choose to follow His guidelines and walk in the freedom He won for you through the sacrificial death of His Son, your Savior, Jesus Christ.

1. Strengthen Your Freedom with Fellowship

God never intended that we live the Christian life alone. That's why He created the church.

- In Hebrews 10:25 and 3:13, what are believers called to do?

- What can happen when we worship, pray, and study God's Word together? What has happened to you and your walk of faith when you have done so? And what has happened when you haven't?

- How has having good friends who are brothers and sisters in the Lord helped you in your walk of faith? Or how could such friends help you?

- How are you involved in your church? Is God calling you to get more plugged in to your youth group? What will you do in response to this call?

If we avoid going to church and meeting with other Christians, we become weak and vulnerable to the enemy's attacks. But when we worship, pray, and study God's Word together, we are able to build one another up in our faith.

2. Strengthen Your Freedom by Studying God's Word

The primary way to get to know God is to get to know His Word, the Bible. Reading God's Word, studying it, and memorizing key verses will help guarantee your freedom in Christ.

- According to Ezra 7:10, what is one reason why Ezra was greatly used by God?

- Evaluate your Bible study or quiet time.

  — What could you do to be more faithful?

  — What time is best for you to read and study the Bible? What place is best for you? What format is best for you?

  — Who can you go to for guidance and direction?

  — What is the first step you'll take to improve your Bible study time?

In 2 Timothy 2:15, you are instructed to "be diligent to present yourself approved to God as a workman who does not need to be ashamed, handling accurately the word of truth." No one can do this for you.

3. Strengthen Your Freedom
Through Daily Prayer

Proverbs 15:8 tells us that God "delights in the prayers of his people" (TLB). And because of the relationship with God which Christ's death on the cross made possible, we are free to go before God on our own whenever we want to.

- Do you talk to God about anything and everything? What areas of your life do you hesitate to bring before Him?

- Do you talk to God anytime and anywhere? What keeps you from staying in touch with Him throughout the course of your day?

- Review the three sample prayers found on pages 216-218 in the text.

  — What did you learn about prayer from these examples?

  — Which lines will you make a regular part of your own prayers?

Commit yourself to talk to God every day, not just during your quiet time but anytime.

4. Strengthen Your Freedom
by Taking Every Thought Captive

If you want to stay free in Christ, you must assume responsibility for your thought life. Taking every thought captive to the obedience of Christ (2 Corinthians 10:5), you must reject the lies, choose the truth, and stand firm in your position in Christ.

- What is God calling you to do through Philippians 4:8,9? Be specific.

- What aspect of taking every thought captive do you most struggle with?

- What will you do about the struggle(s) you just identified? Who will you talk to about your struggle and, in turn, receive encouragement and prayer?

Remember, you are not trying to dispel the darkness. You are trying to turn on the light, and you do so by choosing the truth whenever a lie comes your way.

5. Strengthen Your Freedom
by Understanding Who You Are in Christ

You will grow in freedom as you continue to better understand and more fully accept your identity and worth in Christ. And you can do that by filling your mind with the truth from God's Word about the acceptance, security, and significance which is yours in Christ.

- Read aloud the affirmations listed under "Who Am I?" (pages 220-222). Write out the two or three truths which give you the strength you need today. Memorize them as well as the verses they are based on.

- Now read aloud the affirmations listed under "Since I am in Christ, by the grace of God . . ." (pages 222-225). Again, write out the two or three truths which are most meaningful to you today. After you've memorized your "Who Am I?" statements and verses, memorize these.

- What can you learn about yourself from the "Who Am I?" and "Since I am in Christ, by the grace of God . . ." lists? How did you feel about yourself after reading about who you are in Christ? What do you understand more clearly as a result of reading these statements? What do you better understand about your ability to be free from Satan and his demons?

Turn to the "Who Am I?" and "Since I am in Christ" statements—especially the ones you are memorizing—whenever you are involved in spiritual conflict. Let these truths about your scriptural identity and position in Christ form the foundation for your freedom in Him.

6. Strengthen Your Freedom Through Sharing Your Faith

As one of God's children, you have the privilege and responsibility of telling others how you came to know Jesus as Savior and how you came to experience your freedom in Christ.

- How are you and the Holy Spirit partners when it comes to sharing your faith? What is your job and what is His?

- Which non-Christian friends can you be praying for? Make a list—and pray!

- Which Christian friends aren't experiencing freedom in Christ? Add their names to your prayer list.

- How do you feel when you think about sharing your faith? Are those feelings from God or from Satan? What will you do with them?

Successful witnessing is simply going to other people in the power of the Holy Spirit and confidently sharing with them the truths of the Bible. It's telling them how you came to know Christ and found your freedom in Him.

A Step toward Freedom

- Read Hebrews 10:23-25. What instruction do you find here? What encouragement for the life of freedom do you find in these verses?

- Thank God for sending His Son to be your Bondage Breaker.... Thank Him for His written Word which presents the truth ... and His Spirit who guides and directs. Thank God for what you have learned in this book....

  Then share with God your concerns about your walk of faith. Acknowledge areas of vulnerability you are aware of. Ask Him to be with you in your battles against Satan and his demons....

  Close with thanksgiving and praise for your Savior and Bondage Breaker ... and let your words encourage you in your walk of faith. After all, God has given you all you need to win the battle for the mind and to walk in freedom.

Again, it is our hope that, through this book and this study guide, you have come to know better Jesus Christ the Bondage Breaker and that, through Him, you have been set free—free to be yourself and free to grow in Christ. Know that He will always be there for you so that you can stay free in Him.

About the Authors

Neil Anderson is the president of Freedom in Christ Ministries. He is a highly sought counselor and conference speaker on spiritual conflict. In addition to the bestselling *The Bondage Breaker*, Neil has also written *A Way of Escape, The Seduction of Our Children,* and *Victory Over the Darkness.*

Dave Park is the director of Freedom in Christ Youth Ministries and the coauthor with Neil of *Stomping Out the Darkness,* a youth edition of *Victory Over the Darkness.*

Freedom in Christ Conducts Conferences!

Freedom in Christ Ministries is an interdenominational, international, Bible-teaching church ministry which exists to glorify God by equipping churches and mission groups, enabling them to fulfill their mission of establishing people free in Christ. Thousands have found their freedom in Christ; your group can too! Here are some conferences your community can host which would be led by Freedom in Christ staff:

Living Free in Christ
(a seven-day Bible conference on resolving personal and spiritual conflicts)

Spiritual Conflicts and Counseling
(a two-day advanced seminar on helping others find freedom in Christ)

Setting your Church Free
(a leadership conference on corporate freedom for churches, ministries, and mission groups)

Breaking the Chains
(a young adult conference for college age, singles, and young marrieds)

Stomping Out the Darkness
(a youth conference for parents, youth workers, and young people)

Setting your Youth Free
(an advanced seminar for youth pastors, youth workers, and parents)

The Seduction of Our Children
(a seminar for parents and children's workers wanting to lead children to freedom in Christ)

Resolving Spiritual Conflicts and Cross-Cultural Ministry
(a conference for leaders, missionaries, and all believers desiring to see the Great Commission fulfilled)

The above conferences are also available on video and audio cassettes. To order these and other resources, write or call us.

To host a conference write us at:

Freedom in Christ Ministries
491 East Lambert Road
La Habra, CA 90631
Phone: 310-691-9128   Fax: 310-691-4035

More Resources from Neil Anderson and Freedom in Christ to help you and those you love find freedom in Christ

Books

Victory Over the Darkness
The Bondage Breaker
Helping Others Find Freedom
   in Christ
Released from Bondage
Walking in the Light
A Way of Escape
Setting your Church Free
Living Free in Christ
Daily in Christ
The Seduction of Our
   Children
Spiritual Warfare
Stomping Out the Darkness
   (Youth)
The Bondage Breaker Youth
   Edition
To My Dear Slimeball

Personal Study Guides

Victory Over the Darkness
   Study Guide
The Bondage Breaker
   Study Guide
Stomping Out the Darkness
   Study Guide
The Bondage Breaker
   Youth Edition Study Guide

Teaching Study Guides

Breaking Through to Spiritual
   Maturity (Group Study)
Helping Others Find Freedom
   In Christ (Study Guide)
Busting Free
   (Youth Study Guide)

Other Good
Harvest House Reading

To My Dear Slimeball
by *Richard Miller*

In the tradition of C.S. Lewis's *Screwtape Letters* but in the language of today's teen, this is a collection of amusing yet eye-opening letters from a high-level demon, Slimeball, to his trainee, Spitwad. Slimeball's intent is to help Spitwad deceive and tempt David, his teenage target. *To My Dear Slimeball* shares how Christ's victory at the cross makes it possible for teens to experience the freedom God wants them to know.

Teens Talk About Dating
by *Ginny Williams*

A book for teens, by teens. Dozens of the most-asked and often tough questions about dating and relationships are followed by short, insightful responses from kids across the country— peers who have thought deeply about life and are trying to live the way God wants them to. Each chapter concludes with a list of relevant Scripture passages for further study.

Class of 2000 *Series*
by *Ginny Williams*

Meet the Class of 2000—young people facing new challenges, tough choices, important issues. Kelly and her friends are fun, enthusiastic, and they're looking for real answers to life's questions.

> *Second Chances*
> *A Matter of Trust*
> *Lost-and-Found Friend*
> *A Change of Heart*
> *Spring Fever*